MW01716678

To Answer the Question, To Find Air Here On Earth

Robert Bennett

To Answer the Question, To Find Air Here On Earth

LETTERS TO THE WOMEN I LOVE

TATE PUBLISHING
AND ENTERPRISES, LLC

Published by Tate Publishing & Enterprises, LLC
127 E. Trade Center Terrace | Mustang, Oklahoma 73064 USA
1.888.361.9473 | www.tatepublishing.com

Tate Publishing is committed to excellence in the publishing industry. The company reflects the philosophy established by the founders, based on Psalm 68:11,

"The Lord gave the word and great was the company of those who published it."

Cover design by Lirey Blanco
Interior design by Jomar Ouano

Published in the United States of America

ISBN: 978-1-68207-061-1
Family & Relationships / General
15.10.01

To all of the women who have played any role in my life over the last several years. I especially want to thank those hurting women who allowed me to learn how to help them while simultaneously helping me to become a better man!

ACKNOWLEDGMENTS

I wish to express my deepest appreciation to my friend Verona Moody, for her constant support, encouragement, and tireless energy in making sure I stayed focused on completing this book.

To my lovely daughter, Lyria, who helped me to believe in happily ever after again.

To Donald Schultz, for taking a risk to appoint me as the first male program director of an all-women facility in Western, New York, which has allowed me to blossom to this point in my life.

To my mother, Annie Whigham, for teaching me always to follow my dreams.

To the Western New York Women's Substance Abuse Services Network, for allowing me to join their organization as we strive together to enhance services for hurting women and their children.

To the staff of FHI Madonna House, thank you for trusting, believing, and loving me while I learned to help hurting women.

FOREWORD

Suave, laid-back, honest, sincere—these are just a few words to describe Rob Bennett. Rob can caress you with his gentle mannerisms and at the same time be direct and to the point. His criticisms are not biting, and his opinions are nonjudgmental.

Rob Bennett's advocacy for women clearly shows in his work. His book exposes his heart and allows the reader to peer into his soul. Those who read Rob's work will walk away hoping that someday, someone will write a letter about them.

Working in the field of domestic violence and victim advocacy for more than twenty years, I thought I had some insight on what works best when dealing with women that have experienced violence, alcohol and/or drug addiction, and mental illness—all which frequently go hand in hand. Low-self-esteem issues are usually high on the "problem ladders" as are poor choices for women that have experienced these issues. In 2006, I learned that a women's housing program I frequently collaborated with was hiring a male to supervise this all-women's program. My immediate thought was, *What are they thinking?* At a meeting several weeks later, I noticed a new face in the crowd. It wasn't hard to miss as it was the only male face in a room of fifteen women. This was my introduction to Rob Bennett.

Through the nearly four years that I have known Rob, I have watched him change this women's program into one of the most successful programs in the county. Through his gentle guidance, caring support, and strength and encouragement, women who at one time might have been considered to be lost are now flourishing into radiant, proud individuals, with new goals and dreams for themselves.

Even his staff has changed. They have grown into confident, self-assured professionals who have learned how to take control and yet are comforting and encouraging. Whenever the staff or residents speak about the program, Rob, or something he's done, their whole faces light up. That's the kind of guy Rob is.

When reading his book *Letters to the Women, I Love*, you almost feel as if you are intruding on his inner thoughts. Here he is, exposing his heart and soul, allowing the reader to peer inside. Most men hide their emotions; Rob puts them out there for all to see. After reading this book, women from all over and from every age will be hoping that someday, someone will write a letter to them or about them like Rob has done.

—Cheryl Blacklock
Executive Director
Niagara County Mental Health Association

INTRODUCTION

Agape

The use of this word describes the fatherly *love* of God for humans and their reciprocal *love* for God. The term extends to the *love* of one's fellow human.

It was just like any other ordinary night; nothing unusual was going on, and I had not just return from some retreat or spent any time committed to some meditation. I was feeling bored and a little tired, so I lay down for a quick nap; this was when I believe God showed me a book to write. While it was very evident to me that I was to write this book, at the time I received the vision, I thought the book would be about a total different subject. I had no idea that I would be going on an adventure that would ultimately change my life and thought process as the words flowed across the pages.

The Dream (Vision)

The book was beautiful; it contained the faces of four women on the cover. The background was an autumn color, and it looked as if the sunrise was coming up from behind the women. I saw nothing else going on in the dream but the picture of this book containing a title that was very clear: *To Answer the Question, to Find Air Here on Earth.* Although puzzled at the time, I thought the book would be about four female basketball players. I didn't know any female basketball players, which made this image even more confusing to me. Although all this was strange, I realized that I would be writing about women, but the subject material would not be basketball.

As to the title—in a conversation with one of my female friends, she told me the image of basketball players stood for something that I loved. She also referred to the talent involved in playing the game. The word *air* stood for knowledge, so the dream was letting me know that I was seeking knowledge about individuals that are talented, and who I love. It was at this moment that I realized I was being shown a book that I would write about women detailing my past three years of experience with them.

Some of these women have been my allies, some casual friends, some enemies, and some confidants. I have hated, applauded, envied, and wondered about them; honored, adored, and indeed learned agape love and respect for them.

These women have been very special to me and have become a very integral part of my development.

They forgave me for not seeing their real value in the past and have been women in which I could totally be authentic. They have prayed for me, let me vent, comforted me with their words, inspired me, made me anxious, left me speechless, let me babble, and made me babble. Many of them have been my closest female friends, and I love them very much. Most of all, *they* are responsible for making me the *man* I am today.

I do not know where this book will take me. As I journal my deepest thoughts, I hope it will inspire women to continue to take their rightful position in life while simultaneously encouraging men to assist and support women in the agape way.

I guess the best way to start this endeavor is with a sincere apology to all women, especially those women that I mistreated in my life's journey. I do not claim to speak for all men. However, I would like to stand in the gap as a symbolic gesture on behalf of appropriate men, apologizing for all the atrocities done in the name of machismo, egotism, and selfishness.

Many women experience rape, hurt, misuse, made to bear children while at the same time forced to have abortions. They have experienced abandonment and, on many occasions, stripped of all positive energy by the same men that promised to love them. For this, I am sorry. I know that a *sorry* does not fix all the things that you may have experienced as women at the hands of inappropriate men. My hope is that the words in this book will begin the healing process for you, if this has been your situation, and help you find the real strength and beauty that lies within you.

Before I get into the meat of this adventure, I must give you a frame of reference so that you can understand why it is so ironic that I would write a book of this nature.

I started dating late (approximately age seventeen), and just like many young men and women, it was love at first sight. I spent an entire summer trying to attract this young woman. And when she finally gave me a chance, I got caught like a fish—totally hook, line, and sinker.

I did every romantic thing possible, which included my favorite activities: walking and sharing my most intimate thoughts. Of course, it was puppy love; and I did not know any better, so I was blinded by love like most young men and women when they fall in love for the first time. Just like most young people, it was more infatuation than love, so the inevitable happened: *she broke my heart*!

From that point on, I decided that women were no good unless they could do something for me such as give me sex, money, or fulfill some other superficial desire. I began my quest into womanizing, and I was determined to be relentless at it. My first quest was to conquer every woman that I could sexually. I would do whatever it took to "get it," but I didn't love them. So once I got what I wanted, I was "gone with the wind."

I used women, abused them, pimped and stole from them, degraded and plain-out dogged them. My thinking at that time was a woman was of no real use to me except to use as a doormat. I had to tell you this in its entirety, not to glamorize or justify any of my past behavior, but so that you will understand the irony of me writing this book. It has not been an easy task, and I have received many criticisms. Most of the challenges have been in reference to my making any comments in regard to women healing, and some may continue this criticism after reading this.

It is my sincere hope that you will not take any of the statements I make toward women in this book in a demeaning way. I would hope that any person reading this book would look deep into the pages and find the positive characteristics in each presentation. If you get any negative perspective, please know that it is unintentional and not the goal of this book. As far as I am concerned, I would be the most unlikely man to write a book of this nature.

My life changed approximately fifteen years ago, which took me on a new journey, but that's a different story and not the focus of this book. I may share that story at a later date. Have you heard the saying "God has a sense of humor"? Well, I am convinced that He does, and in May of 2006 God's humor would come to fruition. I would become a program director of an all-women / women with children / alcohol- and substance-abuse residential treatment facility.

Since then, I have begun my reeducation concerning women, and I have started my reeducation about what it means to be an appropriate man. I don't claim to be an expert on women or men, but I have gained some insights that I believe could bring about healing and unity to both genders. I will share my journey (which continues); I hope that it is a beacon of hope to all that will take the time to read it.

There are only two women who I will directly point out in this book; these two have greatly influenced my life, and I don't mind exposing their efforts toward my "male maturity development" process. I believe it is only proper that these two get mentioned. The two women I am talking about are my mother and my daughter.

I will speak directly to them as I journal, but the rest will remain unknown; thus any other woman reading the book will have to guess to see if a letter fits her characteristics or not.

Mom, how could I even begin to think about writing a book concerning women without starting with you, the first woman that I ever got to know? From all outward appearances, one would think that you were just another ordinary black woman. You owned no fancy clothes or car, no major degrees, not a lot of money, and so on. As a single black woman raising five children in the '70s, you were supposed to raise thugs, whores, and underachievers. Instead, you raised brilliant and talented individuals, unique, and not just more negative statistics.

Mother, you cannot measure your *greatness*. Your ability to *instill hope* in me and the thought process that *there was not anything I could not achieve*. Your insight has been a precious gift. You also instilled in me faith in God, which has carried me to this point in my life. You were the first woman to teach me how to communicate on a deeper level than most men. I remember how you would talk to me about all types of things pertaining to life; especially what a *man* is supposed to be. You were compassionate, but also tough when necessary. You were a disciplinarian and a comforter.

Most of all, you are a person who knows about *sacrifice and hard work*. I will never forget any of it, especially the way in which you did this with many odds against you. My hope for you is if you ever get a chance to read this book, you will understand your life's success. It is my hope that you are entirely healed by this knowledge, and I hope that you realize how much you helped me find my purpose.

The success that I have been able to achieve is because of putting God first and then the effort and courage that you have displayed while raising me. I have never forgotten the lessons that I learned from you. No matter what accolades I achieve in life, I remember the most important thing that you have taught me: you taught me to be a *real man*!

The next woman that has been very inspirational to me is my daughter, Lyria, and at the time of this writing, love of my life (next to God), you are only six years old now; so if you ever take the time to read this book, it will probably be in the future. The first thing that I want you to know is that I have always loved you. From the beginning, there was never a time in which I didn't want you. *I always wanted you!* You were never a mistake but always a blessing to me.

You may not remember this, but there are two definite times in my male maturity development process that you played a vital role. You arrived in one of the darkest periods of my life and helped me through one of the bleakest journeys I had to face. The first time that you affected me in such a profound manner was during your birth. I was not handling transitioning from being self-centered to being *selfless* well, but then you arrive in my life.

I can see your birth as vivid as the day it happened; you were the most beautiful sight I had ever seen, and I have been in love with you ever since that moment. *You brought me back to reality*, grounded me (when I had been acting quite ugly), gave me the strength to change, and made me want to change to be a better man. For that, I am forever grateful.

The second time is when my life came to a devastating halt and my heart shattered into a thousand pieces. Sometimes you never know how God will use you to help someone else. You were always such a princess, and you forced me to watch every Barbie and Prince Charming movie that existed (*a true love's kiss)*! I did not realize at the time what impact those fairy-tale adventures would have on my healing process, but I am so glad that you were a "girly" girl.

You made me laugh when all I felt like doing was crying. You made me *act polite* when all I felt like was acting mean. *You taught me how to go set aside my own "stuff"* to see the greater need: you. I am sitting here with tears in my eyes because I am so grateful for you. You comforted me and gave me hope again. *You made me believe in fairy tales and happily ever after.* You have been a source of joy, strength, hope, peace, and security; but most of all, you have been "daddy's little girl." And I love you very, very much.

I want to remind you again that I won't name any other woman in this book, but I hope you will find that you share some of the positive characteristics detailed across the pages. Some may even believe that these characteristics fit you precisely.

In either circumstance, I hope that each presentation causes you to do some self-reflection and inspires you to push forward to your dynamic destiny. As for the men who take the journey toward male maturity development, it is my hope that you learn from some of the mistakes I have made and possibly reevaluate some of your thinking. I hope the letters will inspire you to become the best man possible.

Letter 1

Okay, let's get started. I can't say that I know what the result of this journey will be, but I know I am supposed to take it. This first letter speaks to men's role in particular in women's lives and to women who may have experienced this scenario.

Some women who enter your life are there for the purpose of you helping them and nothing else. As men, we sometimes forget this fact when we are encountering certain women. Sometimes we simply get caught up in our desires and forget that everything is not about us. Getting caught up seemed to be my case, and it was when I was at the peak of my game; I so focused on my swagger that I forgot the task at hand. Just like clockwork, it seemed like I met women while they were in the transitional seasons of their lives.

I reached out with the intention of helping these women, but I was not careful, so the relationship turned into something that I did not intend. Here was my problem: these women were still in their process of healing and completion, but I began pursuing them in a selfish way. To be honest, it wasn't about them; I realize now that I was just trying to satisfy my ego and possible loneliness.

When I forgot my purpose for coming into these women's lives, I ended up going on an adventure, and I mean I went on "an adventure." Every time my ego led me, opposed to my purpose, the best and the worst came out of me. Driven by ego, the women that were supposed to become my greatest sources of joy became my most primary sources of pain.

Ultimately they became the catalyst that God would use to change my whole way of thinking. I am not sure if it is harder for women to heal emotionally as men. When I asked some of my female friends, they told me it's not harder for women to recover, just different. I remember making women promises; I claimed that I was willing to overlook areas of real concern only to get angry because those concerns exploded all over the place. Just be clear about this one thing—it was my responsibility to clean up the mess.

Wounded women need genuine help without strings attached, or as a man, you will just add more wounds to an already damaged vessel. As a man, if you don't plan to get your ego out of the way, then you probably should not choose a life mate before she has healed from hurtful transitions in her life. When I tied my heart in a nonagape way to women who had not completed harmful changes in life, I had to dodge shrapnel continually. Even when I did not mean to cause explosions, the pieces from their already-shattered hearts flew at me.

It takes a special kind of compassion and God's strength to begin to be a conduit of healing for women that are in this stage of their process. As a man, if you cross the line with women that you are only supposed to help, you will find yourself struggling with many issues and be on a head-on collision for destruction.

I have done this on many occasions, often to my detriment. I now recognize the women I didn't display appropriate love to were the women who taught me the greatest lesson of all: *how to love women unconditionally!*

When faced with the fruit of the seeds that I had sown, I could have harvested hate, but I have learned that forgiveness is much more powerful than hate. Kindness is far better than being harsh, and compassion and mercy are essential ingredients needed if I am ever to enter into the fullness of male maturity development.

Many women need healing, and if they experienced "twisted love," then it may cause them to struggle with their definitions of *love*. I have placed myself in situations like this with women, which resulted in me displaying a hurtful type of love opposed to a helpful form. Displaying appropriate agape love has always been my real intention since my transformation. These women have taught me to examine whether I am giving selfish love or agape love, and for this I am truly grateful.

If you are a woman who has experienced this type of scenario in your contact with me, I hope that you will forgive me for not helping you when you needed unselfish love the most. I apologize for putting my selfish desires first rather than in looking at what you needed. I helped you to go backward instead of make the progress that should have happened as a result of you coming in contact with me.

I truly have no bitterness against you for any harm that I may think you have caused me, and my hope is for you to develop a real relationship with God. God is the only one that can make you complete, and then you can pursue your purpose and be the woman that you were designed to be.

Any other woman who may have experienced this type of relationship—I want you to know that there are men who will truly love you with no strings attached or any other hidden motive.

You don't have to shut all men out due to a few bad experiences. Take the time that is necessary to complete the transitions in your life before stepping into new adventures. My hope is that you obtain every good thing that life has to offer. I have nothing but love and respect for you.

LETTER 2

These women made me want to pull back from forming any relationship with them whatsoever. In the past, I have felt intimidated by women with strong personalities. I took the wrong perspective with these women, and my first response was to become indignant. When I first met them, I thought, *Who in the heck do they think they are?* In my indignation, I thought, *These winches don't know who I am, and I am going to help bring them down a few notches.* It's humiliating to me now because these women became my real confidants and closest friends.

What I am learning is these women do not have arrogant personalities but are very confident (and often don't hesitate to display this trait). Their confidence is what makes them unique. These women fought for me when others overlooked me and listened to me when others turned a deaf ear. They reassured me when others tried to tear me down and also showed me the humor in my downfalls, which helped me to heal quicker.

They reminded me that I am a good, honorable, and spiritual man. I never know why God sends people my way, but it is clear to me that He put them in my path to help me improve as a person. However, I also learned that sometimes the most confident woman needs "no motive" affirmation from a man (even though I know some would argue me to the death about this statement). Women possessing this personality have taught me how strong women handle business, and I love the manner in which they carry themselves.

I want you all to know that I highly respect the way in which you model strength to women. I believe you understand what women often come up against trying to thrive in society. Your courage to be "real" about what defines an appropriate male inspires me. It is my hope that you come to the full knowledge of the God in which you confess and that you will rest in His arms as you continue to fulfill your purpose in life. I love you very much!

LETTER 3

When I met women who possessed these personalities, I knew right away that they had not yet become sufficiently confident in the strength they possess. They have all the ability in the world but often placed themselves in a position that shows humility, because they believe anything else will come off as displaying arrogance.

In my heart of hearts, I'm not sure if they liked me on the first time we came into contact with each other. I know the issue is trusting. I understand why women take such a position; women get placed in positions in which they have to discern a man's motives for helping them. Discerning motive becomes especially true if it challenges women to make choices that could have the potential to explode in their faces.

Often, for women to trust a man is a very tricky position to navigate, but I am happy when women don't shut out all men in the face of these odds. Women possessing these personalities have so many characteristics that I honor and respect that it would take forever to talk about in one book, so I will just highlight a few.

You all love when you're needed, but you are firm when necessary. You are quiet and not boastful, but know when to be demanding when it comes to battling for what is right. I watched you women display great courage as you traveled into the future with men, especially when you had to trust that you are not getting led in the wrong direction.

These women always prove to be great assets. As they push to new levels of thinking, they are forced to take greater risk. I say this because you are loyal. And to follow your heart may mean breaking long-standing relationships. I challenge you to become all you can be, and I am grateful to you for allowing me to offer you this challenge. I hope you believe me because there are so many that think I am just some crazy lunatic left-brain-thinking male.

However, I am aware that some women need a little nudging and pulling to walk in their full purpose. Here is a hint to men: if you are going to tune out a woman, do it when she is fighting against maximizing her full potential. I am of the belief that they may need some encouraging or they may just bow out gracefully, which would serve no one.

If you believe this letter speaks to your heart or personality, I want you to know your impact. You teach how to take a second look before coming to a final decision. You reveal how women process events and can greatly influence men in our interaction with women.

As I continue to develop as a man, I don't think I could ever repay women. My message is that I have complete confidence in your ability to change the world and walk in your preordained destiny. You have so much strength, knowledge, and talent that it is hard to put in words. I want to thank you for trusting when everyone else thought you shouldn't. I want to thank you for backing when others acted contrary. Thank you for taking a leap to pursue a dream that would help many women. I have nothing but love and respect for you.

LETTER 4

In the past, I had the tendency to get so focused on women's "shells" that I forgot to look for the beauty that was inside. Some women's outward appearance made us believe they are hard, sarcastic, mean, and obsessive. But they are the total opposite of what we think. What I have learned is that they are just more detailed oriented and like to stay on task. They are very diligent and vigilant.

When everything in life spirals out of control, it becomes very hard to pay attention to the minute details of life. Not paying attention to necessary tasks can take us down negative paths. Many women protect us from ourselves by making sure that things stay in order.

They kept us focused on task, bailed us out when we forget things, and showed us how to focus on the small things that make an enormous difference. They identify with us opposed to comparing, give us the courage to be firm when necessary while also showing ways in which to enjoy the small pleasures of life.

I may sound redundant, but I owe women so much; personally, they helped me smile again. They laughed with and at me. I even saw hearts break for me when I was going through devastating times in my life. Women were the straight shooters with me, and that is what I needed the most. If you as a woman can identify with this letter, I hope that your life continues to be full of joy, peace, and contentment. I am proud to call you my friends, and I love you very much.

Letter 5

I want to continue with the theme of looking at outer shells, which can be very deceptive. When outward demeanors appear rough, we can become confused and think we are encountering a "better not mess with chick." My first inclination when coming in contact with women with "strong" personalities was to remove them from my circle. I am glad that I do not let my first impression make lasting decisions for me.

In the past, I have been guilty of influencing women in a negative manner only to challenge them to change the very concepts I taught them. I understand how very confusing this situation can be for women. I have watched many women's position and demeanor that make them the brunt of everyone else's issues and watched them still shine in the face of opposition. Sometimes it is simply difficult to deal with one's set of circumstances while at the same time trying to balance role and responsibility.

What I found is that even in the midst of many obstacles, these women continue to be very loving and hate being viewed in a negative light. It was necessary for them to come across hard in order to survive in the trenches. They understand the need to take care of business, but also possess soft and nurturing sides. These characteristics make them phenomenally balanced women.

I watched how women with this personality held back tears of anger, frustration, and anguish. But I have also seen them hold back tears of joy and excitement when seeing other women come into their sense of self. The women who come in contact with you are usually thankful; they needed someone to push them instead of allowing them to be idle.

If you are reading this letter and it resonates with you, I want to let you know how much I respect how you build character. You teach the principle of balance even when it would be easier to act another way. You also show the various aspects of humility. My hope for this personality match is that you will know just how appreciated you are and how much you have positively influenced women's lives. You honor us with friendship; thus I love and respect you very much.

Letter 6

I have the benefit of meeting women who share the same insights in regard to helping women. When I explained the insights I have gained, not only did they get it, but I realize that they were placed in my life to help me see the details of the dream clearer. They help to make every line distinct and every piece fit into the right position.

However, I learned one tragic mistake that cause relationship problems for women. We insist they dream big but do not make sure enough resources are available to accomplish the vision. Only now do I understand how very frustrating that becomes for driven women and how it gets in the way of all that they are attempting to accomplish.

These women are brilliant, possessing an innate ability to see the real issues that dwell in the very essence of hurting women. I don't know if this is due to overcoming obstacles in their lives or a God-given insight. What I do know is some women possess an extraordinary passion in regard to helping hurting women. If you have this personality, I ask that you take a step back, to recognize the men who are moving toward the male maturity development process. If you are not careful, you may struggle because it may appear as though these men don't support what you are attempting to accomplish.

It is important to be mindful of when you are in the presence of men yielding to the process of being "males in training (MITs). Past experiences with men can make women have the wrong concept of the position in the process. Misconceptions can bring about a premature death to what is supposed to be a journey taken together.

Every great leader must learn this golden nugget of truth; in order to lead, one must follow; and in order to follow, one must lead. It is a dual give-and-take relationship, and timing is everything. If you have a particular purpose in creating a dream, you must be able to discern this difference. You don't want to act in a hasty manner when it's your time to follow or sluggish when it's your time to lead.

I have learned so much about the journey from the characteristics of these women. The mission consists of good and bad time; sometimes the worst time is having to part ways. Although I am reflecting on women, I caution men: never bring a woman into your plans without first knowing if you will have the resources to support the details of the vision entirely. If you act before counting the cost with driven women, a head-to-head collision is bound to occur.

If you can visualize this letter as a part of your story, let me be the first to apologize to you. Sometimes, men forget to count the cost before inviting you to dream big. Sometimes we don't realize the obstacles women face, so we encourage them to act on the vision before the resources are in place.

Sometimes we don't get the opportunity to chase the moon together, but we do make more progress than we will ever realize. However, I want to thank the women who explained the details that would be necessary to accomplish my vision of helping women transform. Women, you are crucial to teaching men about honoring women and dealing with the core issues that are present in hurting women.

I honor you, and if this letter fits your personality or characteristics, I hope one day you will get to see every detail of your dreams come to fruition. You are a game changer, and you change many minds. Continue to press forward to the full realization of your dreams. I have nothing but love and respect for you.

LETTER 7

Some women are unforgettable. We can never imagine how much they can affect our lives when we let them into our inner circle. For most people, hearing a man making statements about women in this manner, they automatically think about something romantic; but agape love is much stronger than sensual love.

I have watched women struggle and watched them be blessed. I also watched women go through what many would consider being extremely blessed and how it became a source of conflict. However, I have watched many women still love in spite of the mess they go through. The dynamics of the relationships caused laughter and tears. Growth comes from gaining an understanding of each other on a deep level. It is inevitable that buttons will get pushed when navigating interactions.

I firmly believe in divine relationships; you never know who you are meeting, so be careful about how you treat people. I have also begun to think that life can throw many curves, and sometimes men are the ones pitching these crazy unexpected balls of fire at the women we claim to love.

If this letter resonates in your heart, my message is to always be "true" to your heart. Never let what men do, or may not do, prevent you from being a loving and caring person. You are a treasure here on earth, and your presence blesses the world. Don't ever become bitter, because it is like a venomous poison; you were not raised like that. I want you to know, on earth, there is one man that will always have agape for you, and there is nothing you can do—ever—to change that. I have nothing but the highest respect for you.

LETTER 8

You never know where you may find a jewel. Sometimes the most precious stones are locked away in shells that are hidden in a garage in some lonely alley where no one would ever dare to look. It usually does not seem appealing to most people to look through the "trash" to find a treasure, but don't be surprised when you find true treasures hidden there.

It is evident that many women possess class; these women are always elegant and phenomenally gifted, plus quality is hard to hide. They are a very talented but live in the shadows of the commitments made to love the men in their lives. These commitments often lead to them not maximizing their full potential. These women love so deeply that every time they are in a position to shine end up hidden in the cave of a man's desires over and over again.

I consider myself blessed to have the opportunity in my professional work. However, I often get to meet women who have loved so much outwardly that they forgot to love themselves. It is an honor to share in their process of healing and learning to love themselves. I sincerely respect the sacrifice of love that many women make to be what most men call "ideal" women.

I respect the work these women put into regaining their strength. One of my friends calls them "women with a purpose and a plan."

If you identify with this letter, I want you to know that you teach the world to seek for treasures in unknown places. You also teach us not to disrespect the jewels that may start off being hidden in a "pile of trash." I have the uttermost respect for women like you and the dynamic personality that you are now revealing to the world.

My wish is that you continue to expose all the hidden treasures within you. Remember, gifts should get shared, not kept. Keep pursuing your purpose. I have nothing but love and respect for you.

LETTER 9

Unfortunately, I have met many broken women who have been ripped apart so badly by men that they believe their lives have no more purpose. Sometimes men can affect women so negatively that it causes them to stop thinking they deserve good things out of life. These women begin to settle for whatever comes their way and can no longer visualize or appreciate their inner beauty.

Of course, this is a dangerous place because it often leaves these women in vicious cycles of broken promises and unrealized dreams. These women start to pass this way of life down from one generation to the next. I am often amazed at the low self-esteem of these women, especially when seeing how they handle multiple tasks on a regular basis without breaking an apparent sweat.

At first glance, one can't help but think that these women are a walking picture of *no esteem*, subject to any trick from any man that will treat them nice. Observing them multitask, my thoughts changed to *How do they accomplish so many things? They are very strong.*

If you are reading this letter and life events or a man has tried to "break" you down, please listen closely. You are very special, but you must find a way to be objective enough to look at your strength. A man should only compliment a woman, not make her up. You have love, compassion, caring, strength, and maturity in you, but also reluctance; this prevents you from fully recognizing the depth of your courage. If you feel like you need the help of men, find those who will love you with no secret ulterior motives, no hidden agenda, and no games.

My hope is that you become thoroughly aware of your strength. You are beautiful and have hidden ability. You are a gift to the world, not an accident waiting to happen. I love and respect you simply because you are a woman, and you deserve love and respect. Please allow yourself to bless the world with the treasures that lie deep within you.

LETTER 10

Sometimes, people of quiet nature can be deceiving, and what seem to be hard exteriors can give room to very soft, mild-mannered individuals. Sometimes we do not realize personal strength because of the shell, and we misinterpret the structure of the shell to be something that it is not.

Sometimes a smile makes a big difference. Some women allow their smile to shine through, displaying the warmth in their nature and how much they care and share. I want the women that may be less outspoken to know, your realness, especially when facing the tough challenges of life, is what stands out. Although I recognize that women like you are all around us, I wanted to take the time to recognize your accomplishments. I simply want to acknowledge you for who you are and all that you do.

If this letter rings in your spirit, know that you teach us not to make excuses but to stand up to the mistakes made in life and fight if we want change in our lives. You also show that dreams come true—not in our time but in God's timing and on his terms. I learned this by watching many women and now realize that issues worked themselves out when I yield to *His* conditions and timing. My hope is that you will continue to have success in all areas of your life as I am fully confident you will. I have nothing but love and respect for you.

Letter 11

Okay, I guess as I write about these characteristics, you may think, *Here comes the gripe session.* Although some may take this stance, I want to remind you that these are love letters, not complaint or put-down letters.

There are times when men just can't understand women. For us, it is like driving through a violent thunderstorm: dark clouds, blustery winds, and lightning strikes hitting everything in sight. It becomes very hard for us to believe that they are in our lives to temper us as men, and to teach us not to have tantrums when it may appear as though they are having one. It can be difficult to comprehend that we are not getting tormented but challenged to go to another level of being supportive when necessary.

To these women (and men if you are reading this), not only do I believe you are in our lives to challenge us but also that we are in your lives to assist you in developing. Sometimes we misinterpret your actions as it appears that you simply have a "raw" attitude and "rough" behavior. This stance is such an inadequate analysis of the energy these women bring to the picture, and it took me some time to gain this understanding.

We often use the term *drama queens* to try to compartmentalize women. The term is so misleading in describing their personalities because a closer examination may lead to a different conclusion—that we should not define them as destructive or chaotic but merely women expressing their dynamic personalities.

If these women appear unorganized, it is usually due to them being social beings. We misinterpret genuine love as women acting "too emotional." If they appear very animated, it is because they are passionate about what they believe.

If you believe you are getting judged through the "drama queen" lens, I want you to know that I empathize with you. I understand what it has meant for you to have to fight for recognition because of the accomplishments you had already attained. I also know how it feels to believe that you are not receiving the proper respect that you are due.

As we grow, we begin to understand that we don't have to prove who we are but just be who we are. The lesson I have personally learned from these women is "raw" parts of me are special and that I should not give those things up but polish them so that they are useful. Even if you don't know me personally, we have an eternal connection. My hope is that you will receive the proper respect and rewards for the hard work you have done. Keep being *real*. I truly have nothing but love and respect for you.

Letter 12

Some women who cross our paths teach us about real humility; they always look to help resolve issues. I believe these women have the gift of mercy and compassion. There are few people consistently put aside their issues to address others' issues. If you are a man reading this book, I want you to know these women aren't looking for much; they just want to be appreciated in the simplest ways. Don't forget to leave a thank-you note on the table, make them a cup of coffee, occasionally make dinner, and maybe give a foot massage once per year.

If you think this letter applies, please listen closely. *You are just exceptional.* You have a way about you that causes peace when you enter the room, no matter what the scenario is presenting. Those exposed to you greatly appreciate your love and kindness. The way you move in and out of situations without letting it zap the life out of you is sometimes bewildering. You even temper your complaints with compassion for hurting individuals. You display what it means to breathe the freshness of life, to look at the greater good and still have compassion and mercy for those who may be wrong.

My hope is that you also experience the kindness and nurture that you so readily give others. You teach how to show love regardless of how individuals act; this is very impressive. What you bring to hurting women is paramount, so please never stop being who you are. I have nothing but love and the deepest respect for you.

LETTER 13

One of the lessons I had to learn as a man was the difference between my time to lead or follow. I have learned how to cultivate this type of understanding by being around women. It's also good to know that someone genuinely loves with no strings attached. We always need someone in our lives who will allow us to express the deep issues going on in our lives without being judgmental.

All men need to surround themselves with women who can teach us how to watch for traps while we simultaneously assist them in becoming all that they can be. It is so nice when you have the opportunity to glean a woman's wisdom while assisting her in fully maximizing her potential. It is such a blessing to get opportunities to experience these types of relationships; it is somewhat refreshing.

Those that strongly identify here, I want you to know I appreciate how you share your strength and wisdom. It has not gone unnoticed. In the times when it could have been dangerous to expose weaknesses, you allowed us to be *free* in your presence. As far as I know, you don't take advantage of shortcomings even when clearly revealed to you.

I know your purpose is more than I can ever realize, so I don't mind following when it is necessary. The way you move through a seemingly hostile situation without losing your cool is amazing, and your stance on what is right speaks for itself. My hope is that you will walk in the fullness of your ability. I am very fortunate to call you confidants, leaders, and friends. I look forward to seeing all that you will become, and I love you very much.

LETTER 14

Sometimes healthy women let their frustrations get the best of them despite all the good qualities that exist. It is a shame when this happens because it causes them to get overshadowed by their anguish, which sometimes results in them making impulsive decisions. Making a rash decision in the heat of the moment often has negative consequences attached to it. I wish that when relationships end, it would always be on favorable terms; but sometimes, we all get caught up in the cycles of life. I believe a misinterpretation of women dealing with various stages of life cause people to have to part ways. However, parting ways is sometimes the best solution for both parties because the other option is to have a venomous relationship.

As I think about the topic of women and relationships, I ponder about how women are there for us when it counts the most. They stepped up to the plate when we are very vulnerable and weak. They make the difference in the day of struggle. We should be eternally grateful.

To the misunderstood women, I want you to know your value. I am impressed of how you "hold it down" even when getting misconstrued. Because of your dedication even in the face of the difficult phases in life, I wish you the most success that life can bring. I have nothing but love and respect for you.

Letter 15

Sometimes I never know where or from whom I will learn my life lessons. Sometimes I get caught by surprise and the shell, which appears to be meek and mild, has a venomous bite, or it may be vice versa. Now I know that I am writing "letters to the women I love," so I understand that whoever may be reading this letter might experience some conflict with the previous statement.

It would be obvious to think, *How can you love someone whom you declared venomous?* Well, some women act in negative ways when they feel as though they have no other choice. It is not that they truly mean to work evil; they are desperately trying to get someone to hear them or hope to find another way to express themselves at that moment. Unfortunately, women often have to watch out for those who will try to hurt them.

I believe if we strive (by our actions) to clearly let women know that trusting us won't lead to hurt and danger, they will do whatever they have to do in order to give support. As a man, I don't have to become bitter when I experienced women like this; I must recognize the dilemma in which they find themselves. Historically, I didn't realize they truly did not mean me any harm by their actions. They were merely responding to the event, not me.

If you are reading this letter and believe that you have been misjudged by you actions, I ask you to forgive us for our lack of insight. You teach us to pay attention to the changes in your characteristics that are clues that we may have wronged you. You help us identify our unique position to be a conduit of healing and to guard that more carefully.

The reason I express love here is because I have also mislabeled women as venomous. I am using my voice to correct this mistake! These women teach us to love and to learn. If this is you, I wish you the best out of life, and I hope that you come into the fullness of your purpose.

Letter 16

When I think of these women, my thoughts go to how the past became so daunting that they did everything to hide it. I now understand; we often have such different standards for women, and we never let them get away with the issues, things, or situations that we let men get away with. This can often be paralyzing, especially if that woman has made a decision to pursue her future, as opposed to dwelling in the past.

If a person believes that they will get judged due to the love connections they made in the past, they will often keep the struggles they face shut up in a tiny little corridor of their heart. It is my hope that one day we will hold a neutral standard when it comes to men and women—one that supports the strengths and weaknesses in a way that is fair and equal to both parties.

My message to these women is critical: find men who will love you unconditionally in the truest agape sense. It may be risky to trust and let them into your world, but if you let appropriate men into your inner circle, you will not be disappointed. Let these men assist you in finding personal freedom. I hope that you find that friendship (platonic) that will foster true growth in you.

You are caring, supportive, smart, beautiful, and worth it. You can move beyond your past, but you have to trust that everyone does not have a secret motive to bury you. There are individuals who want to assist you in having a bright future. I want you to know that you can overcome any situation, and I look forward to seeing you become all that you were destined to be. I love you very much.

Letter 17

As a man, I didn't realize how many women had been scarred by their past. I guess I would have to say I had blinders on, but one day, those "rose-colored glasses" were snatched off. I now recognize how incredibly hard it became for these women to gather the courage to do positive things in life and move forward. When traumatic type of events happen to women (whatever they might be) they may want to do better in life but often find themselves caught up in the hoopla of life.

These women are only looking for a way to find a sense of self again. Sometimes trying to break through their shell becomes a daunting task, especially in the face of insurmountable odds. Helping women heal, may tax all of your energy as a man, and you may respond by ending the relationship too quickly, but I caution you to be careful with these treasures.

If you have experienced a traumatic event, here is my memo to you, and I hope that you find healing in these words. You are not a failure; however, you will only realize this by coming to an understanding of yourself. Only through this will you find the balance that is necessary to produce the ingredients for a successful life. I hope that you find the strength to go to the highest level in your development. I love you and wish you the best out of life.

LETTER 18

What a difference a day makes. Many times as a man, I forgot to see women completely. This shortcoming hindered me, leaving an unbalanced and critical view of them on many occasions. They are not displaying their usual characteristics, but I did not check to see if something else was going on that was causing them to respond out of character. When this happened, I wanted to take the easy way out and just cut them out of my circle, but I have learned to be cautious about acting too quickly.

When you face women that seem to not be reacting to their usual characteristics, don't run off "half-cocked." Gently challenge and support their growth, because you will then find an ally indeed. Give them the time needed to vent appropriately. Inattentiveness causes frustration to build up, and vexation often comes out like an explosion.

If you are reading this letter and have become exasperated by inattentiveness, I want you to come back to your usual characteristics: gentle, humble, and smiling. Displaying gentleness does not mean you should not assert yourself; it is just a challenge to continue to be a friendly face. If you are a man reading this, you may probably remain disappointed at women for saying things they may not have meant in the heat of frustration. Deep in my heart, I know that at the essence of these annoyances is a truly beautiful woman. My hope for you, if this letter spoke to you, is that you will find your balance again. Tap into that person that I know you really are and show the beauty that really makes you special. I love and respect you very much.

LETTER 19

Every woman that has touched my life in any form is exceptional, but there are women whom quietly affects lives but may not realize the depth to which they contribute to success. From a man's perspective, I have looked at the flamboyant sides of a woman on many occasions without looking at the subtle low, affective characteristics, which are much more important.

If this fits your characteristics, I want you to know you may never stand out in a crowd, but you will always be a superstar. I want to write you a note just because it may appear as though you go unnoticed. You may not ever pick up on the effect that you have on life. Physical rest is critical, and your commitment to consistency allows many to obtain the most vital part of life "much-needed rest." Thank you, thank you, and thank you.

I do not take these women for granted. If you ever need anything, please let me know. Oops, I forgot. You can be any woman in the world that makes it easier for others to rest, so it may be impossible to repay you outside of this letter. I love you very much.

Letter 20

As I write about these women, I want you to know that you are simply heroes that sign up to a higher order. You fit the characteristics of virtuous women. You are totally unselfish (which is not uncommon) and think on a level that many men only wish they could achieve. The statement is not a "put down" to men but only a "put up" to women. You think outside of the box.

Not everyone can fit the characteristics mentioned above, but if you have any inclination that this letter identifies your personality, I give you honor. You are a mover and shaker and have gone beyond what anyone would have expected to accomplish the greater good. I want you to know that you are such a great woman that my words could not even begin to honor you correctly. However, I decided to paraphrase a famous proverb to explain my thoughts toward you; it is the only way for me not to do a disservice to you.

> Who can find a woman of noble character? She is worth far more than rubies. Her husband has full confidence in her and lacks nothing of value. She brings him well, not harm, all the days of her life. She works with eager hands and is like the merchant ships, bringing her food from afar. She gets up while it is still dark; she provides food for her family and portions for her servant girls.

> She considers a field and buys it; out of her earnings she plants a vineyard. She sets about her work vigorously; her arms are strong for her tasks. She sees that her trading is profitable, and her lamp does not go out at night. In her hand, she holds the distaff and grasps the spindle with her fingers.
>
> She opens her arms to the poor and extends her hands to the needy. When it snows, she has no fear for her household; for all of them are clothed in scarlet. She makes coverings for her bed; she is clothed in fine linen and purple. Her husband is respected at the city gate, where he takes his seat among the elders of the land. She makes linen garments and sells them, and supplies the merchants with sashes.
>
> She is clothed with strength and dignity; she can laugh at the days to come. She speaks with wisdom, and faithful instruction is on her tongue. She watches over the affairs of her household and does not eat the bread of idleness. Her children arise and call her blessed; her husband also, and he praises her: "Many women do noble things, but you surpass them all. Charm is deceptive, and beauty is fleeting, but a woman who fears the LORD is to be praised. Give her the reward she has earned, and let her works bring her praise at the city gate."

Many men will say, "This woman does not exist." And many women will say, "It is impossible to be this type of woman." I beg to differ; I know about these women personally. YOU ARE MY HEROES! I love you very much.

LETTER 21

I pause here to journal about a group of women that were very cautious about letting me into their lives until they could distinguish my motives. They watched me and assessed if I could stand up to the test of being an appropriate male. They subtly picked my brain to make sure that I was not just using my gift of gab to manipulate them into trusting me.

They became my allies, contributed to my success, and I embraced their assistance as they have pulled me toward male maturity development. All men should take the journey toward male maturity. I want to thank these women for being excellent sources of inspiration. You all have taught me how to navigate tricky situations. You have given me so many other golden nuggets that it kept me pure and focused.

We share the same goals and desire the same things; our motivation is to empower women. In my list of women that are heroes, you all are in the top ten. And I truly admire, respect, and love you.

Letter 22

Have you ever heard of the glass ceiling? Well, I have, and I had to confront it right in its ugly face. A woman that I highly respect imparted this piece of wisdom to me: "One woman can change one thing, but all women can change all things." I'd like also to thank this second group for allowing me access to the empowering women movement; this is an adventure that I honestly could not take on my own. Thank you for not excluding me from the incredible journey of understanding when others used my gender to keep me at bay.

I was just a lone ranger before you invited me into your circle. I just didn't know what I didn't know, but I am now open to learning. I know I have such a long way to go, but because you opened your arms, I am well on my way. I just want you to know that I love and respect you very much.

Letter 23

I started this journey without knowing women would become quiet giants in my life. Always willing to look past whatever situation I might have been going through, they still loved me despite how ugly I may have been acting at the moment. They showed me the different sides of their personalities on so many occasions and gave me access to the intricate parts of their world, wherein I also felt I could be transparent with my multicomplex sides. The truths I learned set a very sound foundation for the journey that I am now on.

If I had a chance to do it again, I would listen more and argue less. It is very nice to know that someone in the world is indeed concerned my well-being. I want you to know that I honor and highly respect you. If this sounds familiar to you, I want you to know how important it is to allow others to blossom under your wings. You love when others drop. You teach us to be men of principle, which is far more valuable than gold. You are truly an inspiration, and I love you very much.

LETTER 24

As I think about these women, I can't help but realize what a source of strength they have been—teachers, mentors, confidants, and friends. They leave us flabbergasted in their presence. They challenge when necessary and console when we fail. They allow us to do our thing while trusting we will make the right decision.

They allow us the opportunity to make mistakes without rubbing it in. Anytime we blow it, these women don't lecture; they simply crack a little smile as opposed to saying, "I told you so." If only one day I become half the man that they are as women.

If you find this letter speaking to you, I want you to know that you mean so much; and even when you may think others are not listening, they are hanging on to your every word. Your words shape; they helped men on the journey toward male maturity development. I just wanted you to know that I admire, respect, and love you very much. Thank you for all that you do.

Letter 25

Life contains a series of seasons: spring, summer, fall, and winter. I don't believe we always recognize which season our relationships are in with some women. There are times in life's journey that we catch ourselves doing what we believe is the right thing only to *lose* the right thing. When I think about these women, I focus on how they touch so many areas of lives. Sometimes on our journey, they operate as buddies; people with whom we can be *real*. Sometimes they function as spiritual allies. Sometimes they are simply women with whom we can confide.

I just want to tell these personality types, thank you! There are times in life when we all lose confidence, and although confidence comes from within, there are times when outside forces play a significant role. You teach us to laugh, act silly but also get serious when necessary. You are great influences in helping us to dream, hope, and wish. But not to get bent out of shape when our wishes don't go the way we think they should. I want you to know that I love you with no conditions imposed. I wish you nothing but the greatest success, peace, and happiness in life.

LETTER 26

I am so glad to have the opportunity to meet women who are kind to me. I can't say that I could discern if they were against me, but if they were not for me, I would have never known. I respect the fact that when these women could have taken sides; they remained neutral. It is a shame that due to circumstances out of our control, we sometimes can no longer enjoy the same type of fellowship we once had with *real* women.

I now recognize that some women are destined to be in our lives for only a season, so don't take these seasons for granted. There is a secret to maximizing these relationships, and it is always to try to nourish the connection with energy.

If you are a woman who has lost genuine (platonic) relationships with men and find it somewhat strange trying to understand the new season of your association, understand those links are not entirely dead like the winter. One time a woman I respect asked me a question about the change in our relationship, and this was my answer: "Semantics is not as important as relationships." I reminded her that our relationship had always been one of love and respect. There is nothing that I wouldn't do for her, and I have nothing but love and respect for her. I hope you take these words and let it transform your mind-set about those friendships.

LETTER 27

When these women arrive in our worlds, they light the fires of the creative relationship-building skills needed for us to fulfill our potential. It is like the birth of a child—they bring life, get juices flowing, and inspire us to do and be better. Some men get bent by these types of women and throw them away; this comes across as abuse. Understand that they are here to teach us temperament and how to nourish.

We can't get caught up in the work and time involved in assisting them with maximizing their full potential. If we have patience, we will get a chance to see powerful women take the world by storm. Opposed to pushing these women away, we need to thank them.

If we embrace these women, they will bring out the desire to dream again. Their personalities challenge us to check our emotions. This predicament is excellent for us because it allows for the accomplishment of the greater good in many lives. Their courage to let us see the different (often complex) sides without hesitation moves us. They are playful and rigid at times and also straightforward. They are dramatic, flamboyant, but also very inspirational.

I want these women to know that you help us to be more tempered. You teach us not to rush to shut out other views, views that may take another path to success. You teach us how to laugh and not act out from a male perspective all the time. You help us learn how to use wisdom and think situations through. I have nothing but love and respect for you as women.

Letter 28

As I think about these women, I have to thank them for simply having our backs.

You have not gone unnoticed, and we greatly appreciate your commitment to our success. You are natural *people* persons and have natural leadership capabilities. I understand that you have been dealt with multiple letdowns from men in your past to the point that you may believe you are stuck at a lower level of living. However, this thinking does not match your capabilities. Living a life filled with setbacks does not give an accurate picture of all the gifts you possess inside.

My message to these women is I know you may no longer believe that it is worth exploring (pushing) beyond the limits of your imagination. However, it is my sincere belief that if you stretch your imagination, it will lead you to even greater success in life. I hope you take a risk to follow your dreams. I hope you start to dream again and maximize your potential.

If you find this letter tugging at your heart, please take this little bit of advice from me: never settle for a man that is not of quality character. I want you to know that I admire your toughness and the way you handle business in spite of what life tries to hand you. You are a great asset to the world, and I have nothing but love and respect for you. You are a *great* woman!

Letter 29

Like many men, in the past I had been attracted to the physical characteristics of a woman before I really got to know her. I am so glad to be able to say that I have developed beyond viewing women as eye candy. The women who allowed me to help them to achieve their goals humble me. I honor the position. This letter also speaks to men. Please understand your purpose and position in each woman's life you touch so that you unleash greatness into the world and not infatuation.

If you are reading this letter, thank you for allowing me to provide mentoring to you. I respect the fact that you are open to the wisdom I offer. I honor the fact that you trust me enough to let your guards down even if you don't know if I am trying to run "game" or not. I am learning one of the unique lessons any man should know, and that is shells are just that—outer. Real beauty lies in the wealth of wisdom and knowledge deep within both sexes. You have both knowledge and understanding, and I hope you continue to share them with the world. I love and respect you very much.

Letter 30

It may appear as though this letter is the same as those before. I have run into so many women who share similar experiences from the past that I cannot avoid the commonality.

Some women are so demoralized from their past mistakes they find it very hard to believe they are worth any investment. Life events have so stifled these women they never had the opportunity to maximize their hidden real potential. I hope I can impress on you that failure to reveal your talents will ultimately affect dozens of individuals that will never have the benefit of being touched by your gifts.

Women affect many lives. Societies are responsible for nurturing women back to health. We need to become more successful in nurturing women back to good physical, mental, and emotional health because all of society benefits from this. I have been blessed to have the symbolic experience of helping the caterpillar transform into a butterfly, which is truly a beautiful thing.

If you are a woman stuck in the misery of your past mistakes, I want you to know that you have so much to offer the world. You are not your past, and your future is not determined by any mistake that you have made. You are a wonderful, beautiful woman, and you are a gift to the world. Please share all that you possess inside with the world. I love and respect you very much.

LETTER 31

I continuously find myself blessed to be in the presence of beauty- and grace-gifted and talented women who have been overlooked. Often, I get the opportunity to be in the presence of these gifts when they have been broken and used. It is truly an honor to be a part of the healing process of broken women. It is truly an incredible experience to be able to assist women with polishing their gifts and talents so they can be useful again.

If your experience has broken your spirit, I want to remind you that you have been blessed to do many things well. However, you have forgotten that you have special talents because they come so natural to you. You have a responsibility to share the good parts of you with anyone that you can; it won't serve anyone if you keep these gifts to yourself. Be the best that you can be. Don't sell yourself short, but expose the hidden parts to the world. This stance is where your beauty lies. I simply want you to know that I love and respect you very much.

Letter 32

Although I am very passionate about loving all women, some women hold a very special place in my heart. They remind me of what courage and belief can do.

You taught us how to hope when all hope appears lost, have faith when we are surrounded by doubt, and to believe in the impossible when all odds seem to be against us.

These women may exhibit a robust exterior because they think that being hard is the best way to get your needs met. However, after a closer observation, I got to watch these women move beyond that façade because they have such a soft heart. I am so thankful to these women for allowing me the opportunity to watch them transform into beautiful individuals—women that are focused and have a purpose.

If you are reading this letter and believe that you have a well-rounded personality, I want you to remember—anything is possible, but it takes hard work and commitment. Continue to grow, butterfly, continue to grow. I love you very much.

LETTER 33

By the time I came into contact with these women, they had lost their drive and did not believe their lives could be any better. These women walked around pretending that everything is all right. I can tell these women feel as though if they told me what was going on in their minds, they would not get my help. One woman said if she ever lost what is the center of her world, the motivating factor in her life (her child), then it would become hard for her just simply to breathe.

I can't say that I quite understand the connection between a mother and her child. I feel grateful that she shared that part of herself with me so that I could try to gain an understanding. Anytime we talked, I was hoping that she would come out of her shell and possibly begin to trust that I meant every word that I said to her.

If this letter is similar to your experience, I want you to know that there is hope for you. Your past does not have to limit you, and you can have a bright future. I have often said that you can't take your past into your future, but your past can have a direct impact on your future if you don't put it in the right perspective. You are a success, and you are worthy, and I hope that one day you will believe this. I love you very much, and I sincerely respect you.

Letter 34

I am very troubled as I think about these women because they never had a chance to believe that life could offer anything else but degradation, shame, and abuse. When I heard the details of their many stories, I was somewhat shocked, but I started to hear these stories so often that it is hard to believe that these situations are made up.

I understand why you can't "just get over it." The first people supposed to protect you (your caregivers—both mother and father) took actions that may have corrupted you. Furthermore, every time you opened your heart to believe that someone was on your side, they let you down. I expect for you to guard your heart after experiencing all the trauma you had to endure in your life. I realize that this has happened to you so much that you may not be able to recognize true love anymore.

I have watched these women get caught in this vicious cycle over and over again. Unfortunately, I have watched them gravitate to poison-type personalities, which has led them right back to that lonely room in their mind, the only place they believe they can find an escape.

If you are a woman striving to regain your identity from the impact of trauma on your life, my message to you is that you are not a hopeless cause. You can get up, and you can get out. Of course, this won't be an easy task, but you can find the strength—and you must. There are women waiting in the wings that need to believe that there is hope for them. You have already endured with strength, courage, leadership, passion, and compassion. You also have wisdom and perseverance.

I want you to know that I love you very much, and I hope that you find your way back to faith, purpose, and love. I honor and respect you, and if you are reading or hearing this letter, my message to you is to get up. The world is waiting for you to get up.

Letter 35

I know that these letters seem to obtain redundant phrases, common themes, and similar stories. I guess this is one of the *downsides* of meeting many broken women that no longer believe in themselves. I have also been fortunate enough to have the opportunity to instill hope within them, even if it was for a brief moment. There is nothing like seeing a beautiful smile emerge from a person that has lived frowning for so long that they lost confidence in smiling.

To these women, you show many sides and are never scared to be real about your failures. You never run away from the truth even when it may cost you everything, and I admire that. I want you to know that you have so much to offer the world, and you are not a loser or any other derogatory statement that someone has called you. You must get the correct image of yourself. You are gorgeous women with talent and purpose. You have a bright future and no longer have to dwell on the past. I just want you to know that I love and respect you very much.

LETTER 36

A long road trip is often an excellent opportunity to get to know someone. Once I had to give a ride to a young woman, and I could tell that taking a ride with me brought up past issues for her because she appeared very nervous. I can only guess that she was trying to figure out my real motivation, and it seemed as though she was waiting for me to become inappropriate.

I believe it's safe to say that women sometimes never know what to expect when it comes to men. What I continue to learn is that when a woman has been stifled by her past, it makes it very difficult for her to see how to move toward a healthier future.

This letter speaks to women who may have lost their way. I want you to know that I am so glad you are moving toward a positive future and are changing your outlook in life. It always fills my heart with joy when women inform me about the events that are happening in their lives that make them hope again. I am very proud of you, and you deserve every accolade from the accomplishments that you have made. I wish nothing but the best for you, and I love and respect you very much.

Letter 37

Often, great women come in small packages. These women fight when everything seems to be against them. I have watched how they physically struggled at times just to keep their heads above water, and watched them push through pain with courage and strength that still astonishes me to this day.

My message to these women is, I want to thank you for sharing your treasures with me, letting me know your secrets, and allowing me to share in your dreams. You are very special, full of courage and ability. My hope is that you continue to push toward your goals and display the courage that you have shown, for this is your path to success. I wish you the best out of life, and I have nothing but love and respect for you.

LETTER 38

When I met these women, they tried their best to con me because that is all they have ever known. The type of *con* I'm referring to is displaying an outward appearance that they are "tough" when in all actuality, they are marshmallows inside. They act like nothing can touch their emotions. What I found is fragile individuals underneath the tough exterior that learned to use their "toughness" to survive all the hurts and challenges to belief systems that had consistently failed them.

It has been so nice for me to have had the opportunity to display genuine love to women so that they can once again believe their dreams can be accomplished. The have incredible insight, charm, and finesse. I appreciate women making us (men) prove we are not conning them (and that's all right).

The thing I want most for these women is to know that you can expose your real personality to the world. Everyone is not jaded or out to scam you, but you must put everything in its proper place. I am not saying to let your guards down and trust every man that comes in your presence, but when you find appropriate men, be willing to let them help you. I wish you all the best, and I have nothing but love and respect for you.

Letter 39

I've had the opportunity to watch the beautiful transitions in many women's lives. Often, some of the superficial messages they have sent were misleading. Some of these women have given me the impression that they were not serious or insightful. The technique these women used was to act as though they were in la-la land; they used this as defense mechanisms, so I would not place too much responsibility on them.

If you are a woman who uses the "la-la" concept as a disguise, I am not fooled. You have charm and grace, your demeanor is pleasant, and people want to be around you. It would be easy to *hide* behind these characteristics. However, in the true spirit of feminism, I challenge you as a woman to take your place in society and show the world your strength. You are hugely talented and focused when you want to be.

I challenge you to let the world know that you are more than just a pretty face. I have a lot of faith in you and your ability to accomplish great things. I love and respect you very much.

LETTER 40

How I wish things can be different with some women, and how I wish I could help them realize how much they possess inside. They are so competent and capable, but in many instances, life circumstances prohibited them from achieving all that was possible in their lives. Some people measure success by the job one has or the money, cars, or homes. Real success is in one's ability to touch the heart of others; these women possess that characteristic.

Here is my message: I know that you may feel hopeless, and it seems as though the world is against you, but you are not a failure. Sometimes, in truly loving a person, it means that you also have to challenge them in the harsh areas.

Some people mistake intimacy as some physical or sexual event that takes place between two individuals. However, my definition of intimacy is when two people share what is inside of each other's core, e.g., hopes, dreams, likes, dislikes, etc. (in-too-me-see). I want to thank women for letting me into the intimate parts of their lives. I want you to know that I love you and deeply respect you. It has been a real pleasure meeting and sharing time with you. Please allow yourself to be nourished and loved. You are worth it!

Letter 41

I understand that these women were forced to enter into the adult world way before time. I realize they got exposed to some cold, harsh realities that a child/young woman should never have to face. Helping these women grasp that being a "sexy" woman does not come from a sexy strut or batting of eyes but in holding themselves with dignity and respect is often difficult.

If you are destined to help women, you may not get the opportunity to teach them everything you want them to learn. When I am reminiscing, I often think about what I have said, inquiring if there was anything else I could have done as an appropriate male to help them see the beauty that they possess. Unfortunately, sometimes there is nothing else we can do but respect their right to make choices.

If you are a woman who was forced to grow up before your time, I hope that there is one thing that I am saying that affects you in a positive manner. There is one man on the earth who loves you with no untoward motives or hidden agenda. That is my message to you.

LETTER 42

Some women I have known for a long time. I have watched their successes and failures. The thing that stands out the most to me is the beautiful smile that they tried to hide in the midst of navigating life. It appeared to me that their smile was the one thing they tried to keep hidden from the world.

Even so, I want to thank these women for letting me take them to a place of freedom, to feel pain and grieve losses they had not been able to. To smile again and feel a joy that they had rarely experienced. It is very unfortunate that we never got the chance to finish the process: the journey of finding inner peace in which we all strive. My hope for these women is that they will take the time to take care of themselves for a change, as opposed to taking care of everyone else, which is how they lose themselves.

It is always good to have selflessness. However, you must maintain balance, or you will begin a journey into selfishness (that is usually how some men respond to having to share the "toys" in their lives). You must take "me time." Taking personal time is not just taking care of your hair and nails or going out with your girlfriends. It is taking the time to look at your inner desires, dreams, goals, self-worth, potential, and defects so that you become the best women that you can be.

I want you to know that your life is not going to be a series of setbacks and failures but a life of prosperity, peace, comfort, and security. I love and deeply respect you and hope that you find deserved peace.

Letter 43

I am so appreciative of these women and how they encouraged me to continue to be an appropriate male. I have learned to cultivate a good fatherly love from the interaction that I had with them. I try to display the love that an appropriate loving father has toward his daughter when dealing with any woman placed under my "care." Appropriately responding to women causes connections that are special.

To be honest, they "push my buttons" on many days. At times, I wanted to give up on them, but God gave me the patience to deal with their complex personalities long enough to see them grow. These women showed me a lot of love. I will never forget the simple hugs that always made me feel like they were biological daughters, so of course, "Daddy's heart melted." Ha-ha.

I address this letter to the women who encourage men to stay appropriate. You are strong women with a purpose and a plan. Stay focused and stay loving. I hope you accomplish everything that you set out to do. I love and respect you very much.

LETTER 44

I try to make sure that I do not fall into the usual tendency of overlooking a woman's wisdom just because they are young. I have seen people dismiss an individual's ability and view them as having little competency just because they are young and have physical characteristic that is very attractive. Men are very visual and often think with our eyes and left brain. We need to engage a woman's brain and not her body parts.

If you are a young woman reading this letter and believe your wisdom gets dismissed due to your youth, I want you to know how much I respect your intellect and hard-won wisdom. You've astonished me with your insight and maturity, and I know that you will do something very special in the world. Being young is great when you learn from your mistakes early enough to change them. I am very proud of you and thankful for you allowing me to speak into your life. I love you very much.

Letter 45

I am very intrigued by transformation. I am blessed because I got the opportunity to watch women transform. I never will forget clashing with women on some very simple ideas that changed the way I viewed situations. I hope to never forget the lessons they taught me. At that time, I did not realize how many women shared particular negative experiences, and I was continuing to perpetrate those experiences. As men, it is imperative for us to be mindful of our interactions with women so that we don't act negatively to their responses to our actions.

Because I am open to learning, when confronted of my behavior, I try not to get in the way. Taking this position has allowed me the opportunity to grow while simultaneously watch women grow. Because of what they shared with me, I have taken another step toward my "male maturity development" process.

If you are a woman who has helped any man mature, I want you to know that you teach us how to step back and examine our process so we are not negatively impacting women. You remind us that everything we do as men will either build or tear women down. For that, I am eternally grateful. I want to thank you for the life lesson, and I hope that you will continue pursuing growth in your life. I love you very much.

LETTER 46

Sometimes I get to make a difference in women's life. I feel very privileged as I think about these women. They were so broken when I met them. They had shattered esteem by words spoken daily over their lives. They remind me of how powerful words can be. I watched them struggle with some of the most fundamental life issues and then overcome these issues and other obstacles.

Please listen carefully if you can identify with this letter. I have watched you grow from a caterpillar into a beautiful butterfly and watched you learn how to believe in yourself again. I want you to know that you have learned how to hold your head high with dignity and respect. You have grown up into the realization that you deserve more out of life, and you can have more out of life. You have taught me that there is hope in brokenness. I love you very much.

Letter 47

I believe that I have been chosen to help women maximize their potential, and with this in mind, I always want to see them succeed. I have to admit, I struggle when I believe that I can't help them get to a point in which they maximize their potential. For so long, these women have been wounded that they started to believe they can't leave their former lives for better lives. I can often see the writing on the wall—mistakes that will come from day-to-day decisions made by some women.

I love women enough to allow them to make bad choices while still respecting their decisions. Taking a step back and letting women make bad decisions is very hard for me, but I respect them that much.

If you are reading this letter and feel as though you are stuck, I want to remind you of the time you shone brilliantly like the sun and illuminated people's lives like the stars. You are a leader. However, as an appropriate man with no hidden motive, I have to say that some women are better off without a man (significant other) for a season. Remaining single is a position that they should stay in until they find themselves and learn that a man should only compliment them, not make them up.

My message to you is to take the time to explore your hopes, dreams, and desires. I hope that you find your way back to that truth so you will once again shine like the sun. I have nothing but love and respect for you.

LETTER 48

You are simply remarkable women. You are diamonds in the rough, but no one has ever taken the opportunity to polish you up. You have shown me so much, and I have been fortunate enough to watch you come through your purifying process. The personal insight that you possess is phenomenal, and I am surprised that they felt that you had to lower your standards.

To these women, I want you to know that I am so glad to see you start the journey to yourself. I am also oh so glad that you are beginning to share your gifts with the world. You are marvelous individuals who will make a positive difference in the lives of other women. I have nothing but love and a profound respect for you.

LETTER 49

By the time I met some women, they have been hurt so deeply that getting close to them almost became impossible. To let me in meant reliving the pain from the disappointments of men from your past, and I can only imagine how unbearable the pain had to be, I want you to know that I understand your position. I hope that one day you will let appropriate men into your world, who have patience enough to help you heal so that you can feel happy again.

I want you to know that it has been a pleasure getting to know you (even if it is only through this book). Even though I did not get the chance to help you completely, I hope that I was able to show at least that if you begin to trust again, you can heal a whole generation. Thank you for allowing me to the part of your life that you were able to expose. I love you very much.

LETTER 50

When I met these women, they were in need of that constant reassurance that they are all right just the way that they are. I had to remind them that they were being dictated by selfish individuals, in their past, who only validated them for their desires.

In today's society, we are so caught up with the exterior, especially in regard to what we call beauty, that we forget to validate all the other characteristics of many women. It is sad to have to admit this, but it is the men who have often set this precedence. Judging by outside appearances has been stifling to many of our women, giving them a multitude of issues to navigate.

These women start to feel so strongly about the need for unconditional affirmation from men that it becomes very difficult to try to convince them they already possessed all that is necessary to declare their beauty. Unfortunately, they continue to look for affirmation in all the wrong places, and it keeps them ending up with inappropriate men. What is so surprising to me is that from an outward perspective, they would probably not have any trouble crafting a modeling career.

If you feel your heart burning while reading this letter, I want you to know the lack of confidence you often verbalized about your outward appearance always concerns me. I guess this is why people are often confused when we look at "beautiful" women. Their outward appearance fools us into not attaching self-esteem issues with them. What I have learned from you is that if all you have been treated as is "eye candy," then the real things that make you up never get exposed.

I just want you to know that you are more than somebody's picture frame. You have so much more to offer the world. It is what is inside of your creative mind that makes you unique, so affirm yourself with that knowledge. I still believe in you, and I love you very much.

LETTER 51

To these women: I understand that you have made mistakes that you can't take back. I mean you have done this by hooking up with wrong men. I call them Juicy, Jelly, Jammy, Lucky, Charming, and Yo-Yo. Those connections do not have to stop you from having a dazzling future. You must gain the right perspective concerning these relationships. These men have caused drama to come into your life, and because of connections (kids), you have to deal with them on some level. However, you can determine the extent to what involvement you will have with them. I hope that you gain enough self-worth in making positive decisions in the face of "baby-daddy drama."

I want you to know that just because you share a treasure together, the inappropriate men of your past are just that—in your past. Always remember that you already have the best part of them. Anything else that does not line up with the best interest of the child/children is just some junk, and you are no longer a collector. You have grown beyond your past and become a leader. Stand up and be the great woman that you are meant to be. You have been set free from your past. I have nothing but love and respect for you.

Letter 52

This letter sums up many of my thoughts toward women. You have always been friends, confidants, mentors, and guides. You always encouraged me to be all that I could be and never treated me *less than* even though you had much. You let me into your world and had been transparent enough to me that I was able to be real with you.

There is nothing in the world that I would not do for you. I don't know if I can express all that you mean, but I want you to know that I love you and very much respect you. Thank you for allowing me to know you.

LETTER 53

Again, I want to say that I am *not* an expert on women, but they have significantly influenced me. I believe that these women are a composite sample of many women, and anyone reading these letters may identify with any one of the letters.

So you may be reading this and wondering *What's the* question *and where is the* answer*?* You may feel as though you were brought no closer to a conclusion. The *question* or *answer* may not be as important as the things I want you to learn from all of this: the knowledge I am gaining and lessons I am learning, which is as follows:

Having hope and believing that there is not anything I cannot achieve: faith in God, what a *man* should be, and how he should behave. I am learning about sacrifice and hard work not just on the job but in the important things in life (my relationships at home). I am learning to be a good man and to continue transitioning from behaving self-centered to a life of selflessness.

To be grounded, to want to change to be a better man, to laugh, be polite when I feel like being mean, and go pass my own "stuff" to see the greater need.

To believe in fairy tales and happily ever after and to love women unconditionally! That forgiveness is much more powerful than hate, and kindness is far better than being harsh. Furthermore, compassion and mercy are essential ingredients that I will always need as I continue my journey toward male-maturity development.

I am learning to put my trust in God and continue being an honorable and spiritual man. That sometimes even the strongest, most confident women need reassurance. To give no motivation as a man and to support strong women as they handle their business. To continue to nudge and pull women so that they can maximize their potential; take a second look before coming to any final decision and some things about how women process events.

I am learning how to focus on the small things that make an enormous difference and to enjoy simple events that happen to be significant events. To balance even when I want to act another way and how to be humble. To never bring a woman into my dreams without first knowing if I have the resources to support the details of the vision entirely. To honor women while dealing with the core issues that are present, love them in spite of the mess and the sacrifice of love.

I am learning to look for the treasure and respect the jewel that may start off being hidden in the pile of trash. To have love, compassion, care, strength, and maturity but to not make excuses for my behavior.

I am learning to stand up to the mistakes made in life and fight for what I deserve. That dreams do come true, not in our time but in God's timing and on his terms. To be tempered and not have tantrums, but the raw parts of me are what makes me unique.

I am always striving to operate from a position of compassion and mercy while also doing my best to stay open to learning. To move in and out of situations without letting it zap the life out of me and to look for the greater good.

I am learning to watch for traps, expose my weaknesses, and, no matter how hostile things become, keep my cool. To stand up for what is right and that it's all right to feel vulnerable and weak at times.

But most of all, you made the difference in the day of my struggle, and I am eternally grateful. Overall, you have taught me how to dream again, so I hope that these letters will have the same impact to you: help you dream again.

—Sincerely yours,
Robert C. Bennett